ELLA'S BRAVE VOICE

DANA FORASTIERI

Made with ♥ on the Notion Press Platform
www.notionpress.com

To every child who's ever felt too quiet to be heard--

May you always find the courage to speak,

the strenght to believe in your voice,

and the kindness to listen to others.

And to my younger self--

This is the story I wish you had.

Contents

Foreword — *vii*

Preface — *ix*

Acknowledgements — *xi*

Prologue — *xiii*

1. ELLA'S TOWN — 1

2. Ella's Most Deeply Wish — 5

3. The Character Who Helped Her — 8

4. Ella's Overcome Her Fears — 12

5. Ella Keeps Practicing Overcoming Her Speech Difficulties — 15

6. She Finally Overcomes Her Fears — 19

Foreword

Every child has a voice-- Some are loud and bold, others soft and hesitant. But all voices matter

Ella's Brave Voice was born from a deep place of understanding-- of what it feels like to struggle to speak, to feel small in a loud world, and to find bravery in moments that seems ordinary to others but are mountains to climb for us.

This story honors those quiet moments of courage that so often go unnoticed.

Ella is more than a character-- She is a reflection of many children who long to be heard but don't yet know how.

Wheter it's a stutter, shyness, fear or uncertainty, this book remains readers that bravery doesn't always roar. Sometimes, it whispers.

And sometimes, that whisper changes everything.

This book is for the children who are still learning to trust their voice-- and for the grown-ups who wants to help them shine.

May Ella's Brave Voice inspire readers to listen more gently, speak more freely, and believe more deeply in the power of their words

Dana Forastieri

Author of Ella's Brave Voice

Preface

Ella's Brave Voice is a story that grew from a piece of my own heart.

As a child, I often found it difficult to speak-- Not because I didn't have thoughts or feelings, but because getting the words out felt like climbing a mountain.

I know what it's like to feel invisible in a room full of sound, and I remember how powerful it was the first time when someone truly listened to me.

This book is for the children who are still finding their voices, and for the adults who wants to understand them better.

Ella's journey is fictional, but her fear, her courage, and her triumph are all real. They live in classrooms, playgrounds, dinner tables, and bedtime stories everywhere.

My hope is that Ella's Brave Voice will encourage children to be patient with themselves, to speak even when it feels hard, and to know that their voice --no matter how small or shacky-- has power and meaning.

Thank you for opening this book and this story. May it sparks courage, compassion, and conversations in the hearts of those who read it.

Dana Forastieri,

Author

Acknowledgements

Writing Ella's Brave Voice has been a journey of healing, hope and heart--and I couldn't have done it alone.

To the children who struggle to speak, and to those learning to listen: Thank you for inspiring this story. Your quiet courage is louder than you know.

To my family--Thank you for your love, your support and patience. You believe in me helped me believe in myself. A special thank you to my mom/brothers/sisters/etc for encouraging me to share my story.

To the teachers, speech therapists and caregivers who lift up children with gentle encouragement-- you are every day heroes. Thank you for reminding young voices that they matter.

To my readers: Thank you for opening your hearts to Ella. I hope her story stays with you and gives you the courage to speak, listen and believe.

And to my younger self. This is for you. Your voice was never broken. It was always brave.

Prologue

Before Ella found her voice, the world around her felt very loud.

They were buzzing hallways, shouting games, and questions asked faster than she could answer.

Ella had words inside her --lots of them-- but sometimes they got stuck. Sometimes they trembled. And sometimes they stayed quiet.

People thought Ella was shy, or nervous or unsure. But deep down, Ella was just waiting-- for the right moment, the right person, the right kind of courage.

This is the story of how she found it.

It's a story for anyone who has ever felt small in a big world, for anyone who's ever been afraid to speak, and for anyone who's ever wondered if their voices count it.

Because it does.

1
ELLA'S TOWN

Once upon a time, in a colorful

blusting town, there lived a little

girl named Ella.

Ella loved to explore, paint, and

dream, but she had a secret.

When Ella spoke, her words

sometimes got stuck like a hiccup

in her throat.

Ella's town

2

Ella's most deeply wish

Ella wish she could talk

smoothly like her friends, but the

more she tried, the more her

words stumbled.

At shool she often stayed quiet,

hoping no one would notice.

DANA FORASTIERI

Ella's classroom

3

The Character who helped her

One day, Ella's teacher

Ms. Bloom introduced a special

guest to the class.

It was Mr. Owl, a wise storyteller

who had traveled the world

Mr. Owl noticed Ella's shyness and

asked if she'd like to help him tell

DANA FORASTIERI

a story.

DANA FORASTIERI

Story Time with Mr. Bloom and the classroom

4

Ella's overcome her fears

As the day passed, Ella

practice speaking slowly, and

confidently

She learned that her voice was unique

and that it was okay to take her time.

Her friends noticed her bravery

and began to listen more patiently.

Ella overcome her fears by practicing speaking slowly and confidently

5

Ella keeps practicing overcoming her speech difficulties

Eventually, Ella's word flowed

like a gentle stream.

She realized that her voice was

just as important as anyone

else's.

Ella became known as the best

storyteller in town, and she made

many new friends.

Ella the best storyteller in town

6

She finally overcomes her fears

Ella learned that everyone has

their own challenges, but with

patient and courage, they can

overcome them.

And so, Ella's Brave Voice inspired

the whole town, reminding them

that every voice is unique.

The End